THE LAWS OF MAGNETISM

How To Build Your Mental Muscles

# Vardan Ingman

# TABLE OF CONTENTS

ACKNOWLEDGMENTS .................................................................... 4
FOREWORD ..................................................................................... 5
WHAT YOU WILL FIND HERE ........................................................ 7
THE LAWS OF MAGNETISM .......................................................... 9
WAYS TO MAKE A MAGNET ........................................................ 12
    How to strengthen the electromagnetic field in a few simple ways. ............................................................................ 14
HOW TO BUILD A STRONGMAGNETIZING MIND ............. 17
BUILD YOUR MENTAL MUSCLES ............................................. 21
    Imagination ............................................................................. 22
    Memory .................................................................................... 24
    The will ..................................................................................... 28
    Perception ............................................................................... 35
    Intuition .................................................................................... 42
    Reason ..................................................................................... 45
YOU CAN HAVE EVERYTHINGYOU WANT ........................... 51
SUCCESS IS HERE FOR YOU ...................................................... 55
DESIRE AND EXPECT .................................................................... 59
HOW THE ATTRACTION WORKS .............................................. 65
DO NOT GO BACK ......................................................................... 72
MAGNETIC POLES ......................................................................... 76
YOU HAVE TO HAVE A DIRECTION IN YOUR LIFE ............ 78
TURN YOUR COMPASS AGAIN .................................................. 80
GO IN ACTION EVERY DAY ........................................................ 82
THERE IS AN ANSWER TOEVERY QUESTION ..................... 87
CHANGING RELATIONSHIPS ..................................................... 89
CHANGING THE PHYSICAL ........................................................ 92
YOUR PURPOSE .............................................................................. 95

HOW TO BRING YOUR VISION ALIVE ................................... 100

ACKNOWLEDGMENTS

I want to say thank you for my teachers in life. Because of your teaching, coaching and wisdom, I became a lifelong learner. Without your help, I wouldn't have published this book. You all put me on the right track. Thank you!

# FOREWORD

Once upon a time, the world was seen as a flat board. There was no such thing as electricity and people assumed that the earth was the center of the universe. We all know now that those statements are ridiculous. The world was round, we just didn´t know it. Electricity
always existed and our earth was always orbiting the sun. We just didn´t have a clue. These things were only illusions.

And that´s exactly where we are today. There are a lot of things we have known for sure about money and wealth and how it´s acquired. We have ideas about abundance and scarcity, about how the universe and everything in it works. We even think about ourselves in some strange way.

If all we have learned about these things from our well-intentioned parents, teachers, leaders, from books and courses and experts of every kind, even from television and the movies, were correct, none of us would be here. There would be no need for it. You would not be reading this book right now.

Everything we experience here in the physical

world is simply the materialized effect of our thinking. We live in a world with some universal laws, which apply to you, to me and to us all, just as does the law of gravity, whether we believe in it or not. I don´t claim to be the ultimate expert on any of this, but I have studied and applied what I´ve learned, and I have seen amazing results.

Are you willing to be an explorer and an experimenter? Are you willing to let go of old ways of seeing and step into the new one? Then start your life experiment right now and open your mind for new ideas. You can accept or reject any idea, but before you reject the ideas outlined in this book, try to experiment with them first. Try it and give it a chance. There is a big chance that you'll find your answers here.

## WHAT YOU WILL FIND HERE

We will speak about laws working in physics and subsequently in your mind. We will discover similarities and you will learn how to apply the laws governing the physical world to your inner world. We are going to change your mind and turn it into a money
magnet. I´m not going to speak about high-level physics, and I´m going to use easy terminology for everyone to understand and apply.

You will discover that you already know the laws but are not really applying them in your life. This book will help to change that. You will learn more about your sensory factors and how they twist your point of view and how they are feeding us with wrong ideas about the world around us. I will show you the real higher faculties and abilities you have.

We will speak about the ways of improving and developing them to the point that you can use them in your everyday life. I´m sure you've heard about quantum leaps before and if not, we will look on them from a new perspective. There is a greater knowledge about this than even just a few years before, so I´m sure you will be as amazed as I am right now. We will speak about practical use of the laws and how to use them properly. There is more to it, so stay tuned and wait for what´s coming.

I´m glad you are here, so let´s start!

THE LAWS OF MAGNETISM

Physics rarely feels more magical than when you first encounter a magnet as a kid. You will discover that laws of magnetism in physics are the same that we encounter in our everyday life. Only think about it carefully. So what is magnetism?

Magnetism and electricity are not only related, but they are also two sides of the same coin. We know that electrons have spin, which gives each atom a small magnetic field. Just imagine a small ball representing an atom and electrons as smaller satellites spinning around this atom.

Normally, they spin in different directions. It's possible to induce the electrons inside certain metals to spin in the same direction, and that gives the metal magnetic properties.

There are certain laws operating in every magnet and we'll go through them quickly.

The first law relating to magnetism is called the "no

monopole law." This basically states that all magnets have two poles, and there will never be a magnet with a single pole. Most people know matching poles repel each other while opposite poles attract one another. We also know that everything in our lives has two opposite sites. There is up and there is down. There is left and there is right. And we also know that if there is bad then there is also an equal good.

Remember, this is a law, working in physics, but also in non-physics.

The second law relating to magnetism is called Faraday's law. This describes the process of induction, where a changing magnetic field produced by an electromagnet or by a moving permanent magnet induces electric current. It simply means that a moving magnet can produce electric current. Now look at your body as a molecule structure consisting of billions of atoms. It means you also have these small satellites spinning around you in different directions. If you meet someone who will attract you somehow or you go into some environment where you are attracted, you will feel some energy there. It means something is moving in you and you are producing some energy moving through you. We can compare it to electric current. We hear people speaking about being electrified or charged with power. That´s what I´m talking about here. You can feel it.

The final law relating to magnetism is called the Ampere-Maxwell law, and this describes how a changing electric field produces a magnetic field. The strength of the field is related to the current passing through the area and the rate of change in the electric field. Simply said, the power of the current and its frequency. It means you can create a magnetic field by letting the energy flow through the material. This energy is aligning the electrons and they are moving in the same direction, which ultimately creates a magnetic force.

Now look at your body again. If you let the energy freely flow through your body and you align your molecules, it will create a magnetic field around you.

I´m not suggesting letting electrical energy run through your body and there is more powerful energy than that. Think rather about thought energy, which is more potent than electricity. So, letting the energy flow, you will be magnetized. And this is the moment when you start to attract. We will come back to this later. For now, understand that these laws are working in you and in everything around us. And once again physical and also nonphysical.

## WAYS TO MAKE A MAGNET

There are also other ways to create a magnet or for something to become magnetized. Among the methods for turning an ordinary iron or steel into a magnet are:
Rub the iron rod with a piece of metal that is already magnetized. By rubbing a magnet over your metal continuously, you are aligning the electrons in the metal in a certain way, toward a certain polarity. The more that you do this, the longer the effect will last, taking more time for the electrons to return to their random or unpolarized state. You are rubbing the steel in one direction over and over. If we look at something, we are changing the flow of the energy in one desired direction. We are focusing our energy in the desired way. There is no back and forth. This is exactly what we do when we focus on the things we want in our life. Not on the opposite. Always forward, and we do it as often as we can. This way, we are aligning the energy and we are magnetized.

Hang the metal bar vertically and hit it repeatedly with a hammer. The magnetizing effect is stronger if you heat the iron rod. We can compare a hammer to some big emotional impact in your life. It means your whole energy state and the current can be changed by a big emotional impact. It is something that will completely change your life. There is a big force hitting you at once like a hammer and your whole structure will change right at that moment. Normally, it is something negative and a heavy experience. But it can change your life for better.

Induce a magnetic field with an electric current. If you put the iron in a magnetic field, it will also become magnetized. It is like going to a positive environment and getting the benefits from it right now. Good and positive environments can be really helpful to change our energy for the better and become magnetized.

The end result of each method is to induce the electrons in the rod to spin in the same direction. Since electricity is made of electrons, it's a good assumption that the last method is the most efficient. This is exactly how being in a strong electromagnetic field will benefit you to become a strong magnet in life.

*How to strengthen the electromagnetic field in a few simple ways.*

To become a powerful magnet, you can increase the current running through the wire. The stronger the current running through the wire, the stronger the magnetic field. Look at your body as a wire and current as energy flowing to you and through you all the time. You can increase the current by connecting the ends of your wire to a stronger, more powerful battery. You can connect to your source and pick a higher frequency to increase the power. This is when you chose a goal in your life which is on higher frequency as your current results. At the moment you made the decision to achieve this higher goal, you jump to a higher frequency, and you increased your magnetic power. This will help you to attract the things needed to get to your goal.

You can also add an iron core to the wire coil. Instead of leaving the center of the electromagnetic field empty, run an iron nail through it. An iron core through the center can multiply the strength of the electromagnetic field by hundreds of times. This is when your will comes to play. Your will is like the iron nail in the field. That is why we talk about the "iron will." Your will gives you the ability to focus on what you want. This focus increases the magnitude and strengthens the current.

The last way of increasing power is by tightening the wire coils. For instance, if your copper wire is coiled one hundred times around a two-inch iron nail, try to push the coils closer together and wrap the wire a few more times around the nail. Doing that will increase the strength of the electromagnetic field proportionately. This is like adding action to your goal. You are working on your goal, and you are moving toward it every day. You are rewiring yourself with the idea and you are stepping forward.

Everything around us is based on these laws. We should learn them, understand them, and, of course, apply them in our lives. I´m sure you've heard before about the law of attraction. But before you can get what you want, you have to become a powerful magnet which will set up the magnetic field which will attract your desired results. And this is what we are going to do in this book. We will change you into a powerful money magnet. We have to do it together and yes, there is action required from your side. Be aware of it and act as it will be required. If you get the feeling that I´m talking about some wishy-washy concepts and ideas, then come back to this chapter and realize it is a natural law. Open your mind and read with your heart. Let´s jump in!

# HOW TO BUILD A STRONGMAGNETIZING MIND

Now I would like to add a little bit of physics again and this is what I learned at school many years ago. My favorite physics professor named it after his special six-stars Cognac. And it was the six-stars rule. Work is equal energy!

Work is done when a force acts on a moving body. Work is done whenever a force moves something. Everyday examples of work include walking upstairs, lifting heavy objects, pulling a sledge, and pushing a shopping trolley.

Work done has the same units as energy - joules. This is because energy is the ability to do the work. You must have energy to do the work. If you do not have the energy, you can't do any work. A person could not push the box (and so do the work) without energy. Work done is equal to energy transferred.

Now comes my question: how do we get energy to get the work done? Or better asked: how do we do the new work which we never done before?
Here is what physics tells us. An object can possess energy as a result of its: position (potential energy) motion (kinetic energy) deformation (elastic energy)

Leave the second and third one out now. We will focus on potential energy and how to gain it.

Potential energy is the total work done depending only on the initial and final positions of the body in space. The work of potential forces acting on a body that moves from a start to an end position is determined only by these two positions and does not depend on the trajectory of the body.

What does this actually mean for you? You can move from one position to another without going through any steps in between. Going from A to Z in one step and leaving B,C,D...all out. This is also called quantum leap. It also means that you can become anyone you can imagine endowed with any skill or talent you need.

Going back to my question of how to get the energy to do it: you have to jump to a higher position. It means you have increased the distance between your current position and your desired one. This will automatically increase the potential energy and you gain your energy to do the work now. Your new goal is feeding you with the required energy to get there.

Now let me add something about energy discovered by Albert Einstein. He had opened up a revolutionary idea that energy and matter are interchangeable and equivalent: E = mc2. (Energy = mass x the speed of light, squared.) In other words, matter is energy, and everything we see is simply a form of that energy. It's neither created nor destroyed but simply changes form. From formless energy to form and into material objects and effects.

In the last century, as physicists went to work with these new ideas, many shocking discoveries were made. And we now know that the behavior of the tiniest particles of matter can be directly affected by the acts of measuring and observing them. We've learned that the scientist
It's intentions and expectations about their behavior can change or predict that behavior. In other words, science has begun to recognize that our thinking, our intentions, and expectations directly influences and even directs the behavior of these tiny units of energy.

Everything which is form, including you and me, is also formless. And what's more, everything which is form is temporary, and everything which is formless is eternal. We also know now that our attitudes and states of mind, our thinking, directly affects our physical health. This idea is now widely accepted.

And because all things reproduce after their own kind, it follows that you are a powerful creator. This is an invitation to discover our own power as well as a reminder of the responsibility that comes with that power. We are completely free to choose our thoughts and actions, which is the law of cause and effect. If this, then this. Always. Now, if either the physics or the spiritual aspects of all this are as fascinating to you as they are to me, you can certainly learn more.

We already have access to this immense power that is within us all, because we are thinking centers and can originate thought, which is the beginning of everything. Read further and start to develop your own power in life.

## BUILD YOUR MENTAL MUSCLES

We all have these mental muscles, but unfortunately only a few of us are using them. Most of us never looked at them like that and this is the reason why we have to change it, right now. Let´s learn how to improve them in your everyday life. You have your imagination,
perception, will, memory, intuition, and reason.

We often misuse these muscles, and we are employing them in the wrong direction. We should understand them and use them properly. We can create the world we would like to live in, and we have these creative tools.

You have to wake up. It will be like finding the door in a dark room and finally stepping up to the light. Life is not happening to us. Life is what we are creating. Something in you is seeking a better life. Learn how to bring the potential that lies in you on the surface and use it for your advantage.

You have the power to create your day. So add these days together and you are creating your life. This is about you and your creativity and about what you will create. If you understand these and find your real power in them, you will like yourself much better. You will be amazed what you can do with them.

## *Imagination*

Everything starts with your imagination. Unleash this power. With it, everything is possible.
It should serve your higher desires and move you closer to the life you want to live.

We can use it for everything we want to have in life. We were using it as little kids. We were dreaming about possible futures. We often wanted to become a fireman, policeman, doctor, or astronaut. We lived in a land of free imagination. Until we get to our educational system and this power was muted. Our teachers in school were taking our dreams away and required us to focus on their lessons. Our imagination was suppressed and not supported any more.

We are still using it, but unfortunately, we are imagining things we don´t want to happen. Many of us are using it in the wrong direction through worry and fear. Think about a situation when you are waiting for someone to visit you. Or when you are waiting for your spouse or children to come home. First, you become angry if it takes longer and after a while you start to imagine some horrible situations and play some scary movies in your mind. You see car accidents, fires, or some other terrifying situations. We are creating images with our mind all the time. There is no difference if you are creating images, you like or you don´t like. Your mind will be working on the pictures you are focusing on. And it will start to look for corresponding images in your world.

You have to realize that everything you can see was created twice. First, it came as an idea in someone´s mind and then became actualized in real life. This is also the reason why there is no one unique picture in the world. Everything is only a copy of an idea.
You can imagine anything you want. So, I would suggest starting to imagine your perfect life.
How would it look like? What are you doing? Where do you live? With whom do you spend your days and how? Only imagine it as a kid who wants to be a fireman.

Through imagination, you are creating your plans. You can create anything that you can imagine. Think about all the inventions around us. Where did they come from? It all came from imagination. Our only limitation is the use of the imagination. Your imagination can connect you to the universal mind, which is like a land of solutions. It´s like typing some word in google and it will show you all the possibilities available for you. You can use this inner internet too. It starts with what you want.

This is how you receive inspiration. Think about this word "inspiration" (in spirit). It is coming from spirit. From nonphysical. Ask for an idea and you will get it. Even if you don´t believe it right now, try it. What if it works? If you see it as some strange idea, think about your way of life. Is it working for you? Are you getting the results you want in life? If not, then try something new. So do not refuse any idea only because you can´t see how it can work in your life. Just try it and experiment with it. Build an image of what you want. Your world will not change by accident or by some magic happening. It will be according to your image you are holding in your mind.

This is also where your freedom can be applied. You are free to create anything you want. So, create something positive. Do not let other people think for you. Use your imagination as your architect of the future and design your own world.

*Memory*

Are you thinking about your memory? Do you know someone with bad memory or someone who loses it? Now let´s look at your memory from a new and better perspective. Learn to develop it better and employ it for your advantage in life. There is much more in it than you currently think about.

Do you hear people saying I forgot that? Or do you say it sometimes in your life? The truth is they do not forget it, they actually never remembered it first. A lot of people think that they have a poor memory and never learned how to develop it properly. We often compare people by saying that this person has a great memory and on the other side the other person can´t even remember your name properly. All of us were gifted with a perfect memory. The only difference is in use and development of this mental muscle.

We know that training our muscles will improve our strength and power. But we often do not train our mental muscles. However, the same principle works here too.

We remember a lot of things in our everyday life. Like our phone numbers, pin codes, passwords or birthday dates from our loved ones and friends. So how long can we remember them? Only as long as we want to remember. So, the first thing to keep in mind is: what do you want to remember?

Memory is developed through easy association. You cannot force your mind to remember something and understand that force negates. So, you should let it work as easy as possible. Only let yourself remember. You can remember anything that you want. Your memory is perfect.

You should study and learn to develop it for the better. If someone says they have a poor memory, it only means they don´t understand it. The sad truth is, this is not learned at school and some of us never learned it in life. If you understand that you have perfect mental muscles, you will know that you are perfect. And this awareness will help you improve your results. They will be better and better all the time.

People usually think about memory as remembering something from the past. Did you know that you also have a future memory? Your memory can work in both directions. It means that we know more than we allow ourselves to know right now. We have an intelligence system built in us and we can work in harmony with it all the time. In the moment, when we step into our future goal, we can download the feeling of having it. We are using our imagination and we actually feel the desired state right now. We can see it with our inner eyes.

So bring your ideal picture to your mind. You can imagine what you want. Now you see yourself in this future reality. Let´s say you went two years from now into the future and you are visiting your future self. Everything you wanted and imagined two years before actually manifested, and you see it now in this reality. Now just say hello to your future you and ask, "How are you doing right now? What did you do in the past and how did you get all these great things in your life?" Then let your future self-speak about it and listen carefully. You will get the information that the current you need. You will get some helpful ideas which you can use in your current reality.

Understand that all the things you want are already created in some other stage or reality. You can´t see them right now, but they are there. You will not have the desire to get it if it has not been created already. This way you can actually download the important information which will help you move ahead.

You can also ask your future self, "What do you know now that you wished you knew two years before?" You will be amazed what kind of information you will get. You will hear that it was much easier than you thought before. Or that you got the help in the right moment when you needed it. It happened so much faster than expected. You will get the support and ideas. This is something that you should use and apply in your current life. There is a lot what you can learn like that, and I actually used my future memory to write my second book. It was amazing, and I was surprised by the precise information I got. I highly recommend starting to use this great future memory in your life. Let me know about it and share your experience with others if you like.

Start to train your memory and you will be impressed by your mental power. You will get more confidence and you will like yourself more than ever. See yourself with a great memory and use it like that. Create a new habit of studying your memory. Develop this mental muscle and you will get what you want in life.

*The will*

This is one of your strongest mental muscles of all. A lot of people think about willpower as some mental strength which forces things to happen. But that is not how the will works in your life. We will talk about free will.

Because of will, you are able to hold to one idea you freely chose. You can decide where you want to focus and let other ideas flow by. You can be in a challenging situation or in some bad circumstances and the people around you very negative. It seems that the whole world is against you and tries to knock you down. How can you handle that and change to another positive direction? You can do it with a highly developed will.

You already know that with your imagination you can create anything you want. Your ideal home, business, health, and your financial state. You are building a picture of an ideal life. Your will gives you the ability to focus on this new idea and let the current negative ideas fade out of your mind. Holding this new positive idea long enough will move it to your subconscious and it will become a habitual thought. This will be the moment when the magic starts to happen. Your new internalized image will move to action, and you will be able to change your reality. You will see new results in your life. You will be in a new positive vibration which will set up the magnetic field and you will attract what you want.

Using your will to focus on one idea regardless of anything else around takes concentration.

When you concentrate on your great idea, you are aligning the energy to flow in the desired direction and you put yourself in a great vibrational state. You are feeling better. You are creating a strong current with your will. It´s like building a highway where the energy flows freely and faster than before. This way, you will get the physical opposite of your image.

Remember what Einstein said. Energy is equal to mass. You will attract it to you.

The will gives you the ability to concentrate. This is a completely different way of using this great power. It has nothing to do with willpower when we try to force ourselves to do something. We are trying to change something with willpower like a New Year's resolution. I´m sure you already know that this does not work at all. You can apply it for a short period of time. But after that, you are exhausted and don´t follow through anymore. You will give up. And why? Because you are not changing the cause of the problem. You are trying to change the effect. This will never work for you.

Now come back to the picture you are imagining. Keep

calm and look inside your mind.

Focus on what you want. This is the moment when you are using this mental muscle in the right way. There is no force applied. You like to do it, because you love this image, and you want to stay with it as long as possible.

There could be circumstances in your life which are the direct opposite of this new image in your mind. Remember, you can never get to where you want to be from where you are right now. You can't get to your dream. It seems impossible right now. This is where you have to shift your focus and actually come from your dream. You can have anything you want and become anything you want to become. But you have to come to the same vibration as the picture you are holding in your mind. If you can feel it and be grateful for it as if it is already there, you will have it too.

You are using your will to establish this vibration, even in the absence of the thing you want.

Take your mind off the problem and focus it on the solution. See the desired goal as already achieved and be grateful for it all the time. You can't focus on the problem and get to the solution. The answer is always to take your mind off the problem and to put it on what you want.

This is what your will can accomplish in every situation. Do it regularly and you will see how things will shift and change to something better.

We should consciously control our mental powers and direct them to our desired goal.

Otherwise, they will only jump back and forth with no direction and cause confusion all the time. Imagination is the creative function, and the will is the centralizing function. It keeps the imagination centered in the right direction. This is why you have to develop your will, which will enable you to achieve the goal. You will move in the direction you want to move.

We live in a fast-moving world right now. There are a lot of forces moving around in every direction. So our aim should be to use our will properly and focus on what we want. Now the question arises: how can you develop a strong will? How can you hold only one idea in your mind and block out all the other ideas?

You have to practice concentrating. I read about Buddhist monks in Himalaya focusing on a rose. They will look at this beautiful flower and concentrate on every detail for hours. They are training their will every day, looking at a rose. You can do it too. When you start, you will perhaps look at it for a few seconds and your mind will start to wander and there will be other ideas coming to you. You have to let them go and come back to the rose and look at it. Let every disturbing idea go. Bring your mind back to the rose. This way, you are developing your ability to concentrate. You are developing your will. You can do it with any other object too. You can even put a picture on your phone and look at it as long as possible without some disturbing thoughts.

If you exercise your mind, it will gain strength. The same principle works with your body, too. Your will is a mental muscle, and you can train it to tremendous power.

Feeling is an awareness of a vibration. Did you ever feel someone staring at you? I think so and the truth is, you can feel it. When they concentrate on you, they have one image on the screen of their mind, which is you. Now all the power flowing through them is directed at you. You are picking up this vibration and you feel it. That is concentration. If you do something, you should be able to concentrate on what you do and what you want to achieve. If you want to be a professional in any field, you should learn to concentrate. Look at the Olympics and you will see great concentration power by each of the great sport achievers. We should learn to concentrate on what we are doing.

The better we concentrate, the faster will be the results. With concentration, we are increasing the amplitude of the vibration. We are adding more power to it. So, if you focus on your goal, you are giving more power to it. You are giving energy to it. You are directing your energy toward your goal.

The sad truth is, an average person can only concentrate for a couple of seconds. You can develop this ability far more than that. You can be better all the time. So, focus and concentrate on what you are doing.

Your mental power has no limits. We can´t even guess what we are capable of doing. We know that laser can cut through steel. It is a focused light flowing in one direction. We also know that thought energy is even stronger than light, so use it. This is what we can do with our mind. Focus, feel and become one with your goal. No matter what the conditions in your life are right now, you can use your will and focus on what you want. Your ability to focus is very important.

It´s like using a magnifying glass and the power of

sunlight. You can direct the sunlight and concentrate it to one point and create heat. It can actually burn you or start a fire. You took the energy, and you focused it. That is what your will can do too. Learn to focus your will. Your will is not here to affect something, but it is here to attract. It will turn you into a powerful magnet.

*Perception*

You are using this mental muscle every moment of your day. You can have anything you want, but you have to change the way you are looking at your life. People normally think about the reasons they can´t change for the better. They blame their parents, school, politics, and many other things around them. They also put themselves down and say things like: I´m not good enough, I have no money, I can´t do this or that. But if they change the point of view of themselves, if they look at themselves from another perspective, their whole world will begin to change.

The problem is never a lack of education, experience, or money, but there is a perception problem. People look at themselves in the wrong way. They should change their perception. They could achieve anything if they change their point of view.

Nothing is good or bad in our life unless we call it that. Of course, there are a lot of things in our world happening every day which we call bad. Car accidents, murders, wars, etc. But you have the choice in every moment to decide what you call bad. Keep in mind that in every so- called bad situation there is also the good in it. Everything in this universe has its polar opposite. Every magnet has a polar opposite.

Because of our mental programming we are usually reacting to these situations. And we are reacting according to our programming that we get from our environment. But we can make a choice and decide how we look at every situation. We can respond to it and look at it from other angles. Instead of jumping in with our usual behavior and starting to panic, stop and try to find the good in it. In this moment you will find your power. You have the ability to pause and choose your response to it. You are not reacting to the things from the outside, but you are putting that aside and creating your respond from the inside.

True knowledge comes always from the inside, so learn to listen to it. You can choose to think differently, and you don´t have to suffer because of your previous programmed thinking. That is really powerful, and you can apply your power all the time. If you change the thought about any situation for something better, you will also feel it. So if you feel bad about something change the thought about it and you will feel better. Changing the thought about it will actually change the whole situation and you will find the good in it every time.

No matter where you are, what happened in your life before and what obstacles you had, you can always change your point of view. This is your true freedom. You can decide how you respond to any circumstance or situation. You can change the meaning of it all the time.

If we get into some challenge, normally our programming jumps out and we start evaluating the situation. Somebody told us this is right, and somebody told us that this is wrong. Now we have our judge sitting there and judging everything around us according to this programming from the past. This judge had unfortunately really distorted point of view. Be aware of it and stop listening to him. If you stop it, you actually find out that there is a You, which has freedom. You can freely choose any idea you want and subsequently create what you want. You can choose your perception.

If you find yourself instantly reacting to some

situation, tell yourself to stop. Make a pause. Keep calm and you will get an insight or better idea about the whole thing. The answer to any challenge is already here. It´s our perception that tells us we can´t solve the problem. Our perception creates our reality. It´s how we see the situation.

※

    Let´s say you want to change your income. You look on your current situation and decide to double your income in the next month. If you look on it from your current point of view, you will have no idea how to do it. But if you had somebody else with another point of view, who is already earning that much or more, he could tell you that there are many ways to earn this money next month. That is because he or she is looking at it from another place.

Think about a time when you were flying somewhere, and you looked down on earth.

Everything seemed to be so small. If you thought about some issues going on, they also look smaller from this place. Imagine yourself being in a big labyrinth and you were lost there. If you could fly over it and look on the way from above, you would easily find your way out. You only changed your point of view about the problem. Sometimes we go through life being in the labyrinth. But we should jump in the airplane and fly above it.

We can raise ourselves above the problem. We can look on it from a different point of view.

Our programming should not stop us from looking for the solution. Keep shifting your perception until you see the issue from a totally different point of view. You can ask yourself: How would the wealthiest person on earth look at this problem? How would the best inventor on earth look at this problem? Once you start to change your perception, your life will change too. So where is your point of view? Are you still in the labyrinth? Or do you exercise the higher point of view? Look at things differently. Let the challenge look small. Change the perception of your situation. It´s not good or bad. It´s only how you see it right now. So, change it!

The frequency of the problem is not where the answer lies. You should put yourself on a higher frequency to find the answer you are looking for.

When you look at something and you are fixed there, you can´t see anything else. We have the ability to shift our perception. At the moment we are doing it, the whole universe shifts with us too. This is when your world starts to change. Your perception plays a big role in your life.

Perception could be also tricky at some points. For example, when you are looking down on a railroad truck. At some point it looks like they are joining together. However, you know that this is not true. There are a lot of pictures on the internet where people see different things on them. So start to think and realize that you have some perceptions that need to change. Look at the world from a different point of view.

You have these great mental muscles, so start using them. Do not let your current perception hold you in the place where you don´t want to be any more. Understand that your old programming is causing you to look at things as you look on them now. Start to look at your life from many other points of view. Start playing with your income or any other part of your life.

Ask yourself how you can turn it to something better. What you see has to do with the way you are pointed in life. Change the direction and your life will look totally different.

*"If you change the way you look at things, the things you look at change."* – Wayne Dyer

The philosopher Plato told a famous story of prisoners chained eternally inside a dark cave. Behind them a bright fire flickers, but they are bound so that they can´t see the fire. They don´t even know what it is. All they can see are the shadows the fire throws onto the cave wall before them. Between them and the fire, other people come and go, carrying trees, animals and so on. But they can´t see any of this. Only the moving shadows. They were there since birth. They believe that the voices are coming from the shadows on the wall. That is their reality.

Now, one day a prisoner breaks free and makes his way out of the cave where for the first time ever he looks out at the truth. At first, the sunlight is too bright for him to see. But soon he becomes accustomed to the light and is able to see real trees, real animals, real hills. Can you imagine how astonishing that would be? To find out that everything you had formerly believed to be real and true was simply an illusion?

Perhaps you have experienced something like this, maybe even by reading this book. I certainly did! Plato tells us, too, that when this prisoner returns to tell his former companions of what he has seen, they will not believe him. They laugh or grow angry, holding to their own perceptions of what is true and right. In a way, we are like those prisoners. We´re conditioned to look upon circumstances and experiences and believe the interpretations we have accepted. We´re conditioned to label them immediately good or bad, right or wrong. We´re also conditioned to believe that our labels are the truth and that other peoples are not.

*"There is nothing either good or bad, but thinking makes it so." – William Shakespeare*

Don´t live like a prisoner in an underground cave. Quit believing in shadows. Change your perception and your world will change. This information can completely change your life. It certainly changed mine.

*Intuition*

This mental muscle will help you get the inspiration and the answers to the questions you are looking for. Once you've made the decision and stated your goal, you will get some hunches and ideas about it. It works like Google. You can ask any question and you will get your answer from your subconscious mind. This is the part of your mind which is connected with everything in the universe and knows about everything. It is everywhere, and it is also a part of the universal mind. We can say that it is connected to an infinite intelligence.

How does it speak to you? You have to be quiet and keep the outside world away. Do not focus on the question. Only quiet your mind and let the answer come to you. This is when meditation comes in play. Find a quiet and comfortable place, sit or lay down and close your eyes. Then let go of any disturbing thoughts and enjoy this calm state. Try to stay here at least fifteen minutes. With practice you will be better, and it will be easier for you to calm down.

Reaching the right state, you will get some ideas. All the inventions are coming from here and every great inventor is using this knowledge. Think about it. All the knowledge is there. It was there and it will be there all the time. You only have to tap into it. You must be ready for it and shut out the conscious mind.

Stop arguing with the ideas coming to you. They don´t have to be logical to you at this time. Look on them as a new point of view and accept them. Many people will ask you: Are you crazy waiting for this little voice? Not at all. It is so different from what the masses do. It is like having a direct personal contact to the mind. Your answers are all there.

Your intuition is your guide taking you from A to B. As I said before, there must be no logic in it at the moment, so remember it´s higher intelligence. Look on it from your desired goal and not from current conditions. What could you do if it is possible? What will you do if you know you cannot fail? When you get the idea than follow it. This is very important, so burn it into your mind. Take action on the idea you received. You will also pick up some vibrations with this idea. It means you will feel it. This is also working in reverse. You can set up your vibration with your thinking and if you think about what you want, you will feel good.

There is a chance that your sensory factors will argue with these messages and they will try to send you another way. Be aware of it and do not let the current circumstances dictate your thinking and consequently your vibration. It will be like arguing with reality. That is when you see a small group of people going in a different way from the masses. So be one of them and do not care what others are doing.

We can also pick up vibrations from other people.

If you meet someone for the first time, you have some feelings about them. You can feel it if it is something harmonious or not. It´s like picking up the phone and getting the vibrations. This kind of communication is far better and more powerful than phones or emails. You can read the vibrations of other people.

If you have some feeling to do something or go somewhere, then just do it. Our intuition does not tell us why. It will only point the way. Everyone possesses intuition so start to use it for your benefit.

*Reason*

What do you think about working harder or longer hours than other people? Will you get better results than others do? Do you believe that working harder bring you more of what you want in life? Why not try some other approach to it? Why are we thinking that with more effort and determination we reach our desired goal? Trying harder is not the solution to achieve more. There is no promise that with this approach you get more in life. This is often also a part of a big problem. If you try harder, there is still a big chance that you will never be successful.

You have to begin to think. And you are doing it with your reason. This is the highest function that you are capable of. You can think. You can originate any idea. This is the greatest mental muscle you have. We already know that we become what we think about. Look at your activities and ask yourself what you are doing. Where are you going and what do you want to achieve? You have to be thinking. I hope this book makes you think too. You should also monitor what you are thinking.

We know that the natural laws are perfect. Nature works in perfection, and we see harmony all around. We have the ability to work with these laws and actually create anything we want. If you learn to work in harmony with these laws, you don´t have to work harder. You only allow the things to happen.

You can change to any frequency you want. It´s like listening to the radio or watching television. If you are tired of one channel with negative news, you can easily change to another more positive one. You can tune in to a new vibration and let the new program come on.

At the moment you start to change your reality and move to your desired goal, you have to remember a few points. First of all, the information coming from your five senses represents only the current state or as you call it reality. This is only a reflected reality. It is a reflection of our mind and the thoughts that we have been thinking. So the things like your bank account statement or what other people think about you, what your history is, what you did or didn´t do in the past has an effect on it. But your future is not determined by history without your permission.

Your reason, however, reminds you that you have your imagination, intuition, your will, memory and perception. You can look on the current situation and recognize that you have more here available for you. You have access to any question you´ve got, solutions to any problem, and answers will come to you when you welcome them. You only have to be in a matching vibration.

You can tap into the universal mind and get the answers about what to do and how to move ahead toward your goal. Realize you have this knowledge inside, waiting for your questions. The reason helps you to understand that. The truth is only a few people think like that. The majority do not understand that or are just too lazy to think about it. People consider mental activity as thinking, but this is not thinking at all. They are usually thinking about the same thing every day. They are not looking for any new thought. They only think as they usually do. They are not using their mental muscles.

A lot of people only live through their senses. They only react to their environment and what occurred to them. Most people operate with mindset. That means with a fixed way of looking at things in their life. They also assume that success comes in one step at a time. It means they can only move from one level to the next one right after the first one. From there they can move to the third one, etc. This is the usual way people function and think about them. They try to increase their accomplishments from day to day. This is how they see their growth.

You should start to think in new dimensions and from different perspectives as we said before. Remember your potential is infinite and you can accomplish anything. Think about the quantum leap. You can move yourself from point A to point Z without going through B,C,D...It means an explosive jump in your personal performance, which is far beyond any logical step. It is something totally different from incremental progress. It´s like multiplying instead of adding in mathematics. Quantum leaps can come without any effort and time-consuming struggle. Think about that. Where could you be if you take this explosive jump? Are you using your future memory or imagination? If not start to think.

It could violate common sense but realize this already works in nature. So do not reject this idea without thinking about it. If you look on your smartphone and what you can do with it today, you'll realize that if you try to explain it to someone in the year 1990, they will look strangely at you. It will look like magic to them. But it is very normal and ordinary for you. Thinking people know that if you can see it, you can do it! You can think.

The Idea of moving to a higher level and skipping the steps on the ladder could sound strange to you now. However, after the fact quantum leaps seem to be practical. But they will not come to you as the obvious move in the moment. Usually, it is in retrospect that you see the hidden logic in it. Quantum leaps are not complicated. They are rather simple, efficient, and timesaving.

Hopefully, this provoked you to think. You must begin to think if you want to get what you want in life. The majority of people do not think. When you think, you tap into an infinite power which flows into your consciousness. Your reasoning gives you the ability to form it into a small picture we call a thought. Then you add other thoughts to it, and you create an idea. An idea is a collection of thoughts directed toward a purpose.

If you have a big idea, you also know that around it are smaller ideas, which create this big one. So, start where you are and add the small pictures to it. Stretch your mind and begin to think about what you are capable of doing. Thinking is your biggest power of all.

## YOU CAN HAVE EVERYTHING YOU WANT

Just because we can´t see it with our eyes, does not mean that it is not there. Everything we want is already here in one form or another. We can create anything that we desire. Thought causes it all and therefore there are no limits to what we can create. Unless we put some
limits on ourselves. If there is some demand for something, you should know that the supply is there too.

We often say, "I don´t know how this will be, or how to do it." But realize what we are doing with this statement. We are already disconnecting us from the solution. Whenever someone needed an answer to his question, he received an idea into his mind. He was inspired by it and then worked on it and materialized it. Why did we live so long without internet and smartphones? Because we were not able to imagine it before. Was the idea for it available to us? The truth is, it was there before as it is now. But there was no demand for it before.

The real abundance of a man lies not in his possessions and material objects, but rather in his consciousness. So what are the things you are thinking about? The things you want or don´t want. You have no choice whether or not you will create something. You will do it anyway. The question is, if you will do it consciously and create what you want rather than the opposite of it. You have the choice of what life you will create.

We often see two people working in the same business in the same area and one is winning while the other is struggling all the time. The first one works only a few hours or less and the other works hard and long hours every day. So what is the difference between them? It has to be the consciousness. There is always a better way to do everything, and you should be looking for the better way. You already know that you should look inside. You have all you need inside of you. Learn to use your power. However, you will never see it with your physical eyes.
Understand that too.

Everything you want is here; you only have to become aware of it. We live in an infinite universe, and we struggle to understand that, because of our physical senses. In fact, our physical senses are only the expression of our internal capacity. We do not see because we have eyes and we do not hear because we have ears. We manifested physical eyes because we have visioning capacity. Physical eyes are the expression of the visioning capacity of our spirit. The same is true for our hearing capacity and other senses.

Our power of attraction was too weak to meet the demands, but only until now. Our mind is like a magnet which draws unto itself its own like type and kind. A magnet can draw to itself according to its power of magnetism that is generated or collected in itself. Our mental magnet power is reduced by our fears and worry. If our mental strength is in the opposite direction, we can even repel the good we want to attract. Our mental magnet has the wrong polarity, and we are pushing away what we want.

As we can charge a magnet with electric energy to build up its power of magnetism so we can charge our mind with mental energy that builds up the power of attraction. Our mind can be stimulated to become a strong force of attraction with the proper thoughts. It also means you have to change your habitual thoughts to something positive.

We can´t use our physical senses and look on current conditions if they are not in harmony with that which we want to create. Looking at your bank account, your health situation, or something else that is bothering you, will not produce any positive thoughts about it. We have to start to work from our mental image and not from a physical point of view. You have to stop worrying about these things and focus on the opposite of it. Use your will to do it.

If you want to become a strong magnet, you have to be in charge of your thinking. So the only limitation is really our thinking and our regular thoughts. What are you thinking about? The more you understand that, the better your thoughts will become, and you will be a powerful magnet attracting what you want in your life.

## SUCCESS IS HERE FOR YOU

It seems for a lot of people trying to reach their goals is something that does not come easy to them. They are working and moving ahead but still can´t see any results from it. They could start to doubt themselves and ask: Is this for me? Or is this only for some few?

*"Whether you think you can or think you can´t you´re right!"* – Henry Ford

The truth is everyone deserves to have success. Everyone has the ability to achieve greatness in their lives. The secret to becoming great is taking small steps every day. Remember there is enough for everyone in this world and you can enjoy everything you want. If we do not have something it is only because we are violating the natural laws. We are not in harmony with them, and we are working against them. Everyone has his mental muscles, and these can provide us with great power to create what we want. We should look on them as our gifts, which are helping us to get to our desired destination. We should develop them properly and use them on our way.

※

In the moment when you start moving ahead you will encounter some obstacles and they are coming to you as a teacher. You should learn your lessons from them. It means it will not be comfortable all the time. And it also means if you are not feeling comfortable than you are growing. And you have to grow if you want to be successful. Being uncomfortable is a part of growing. See it like that and act according to it. There will be some fear in it, but you can overcome it with this new understanding. You should understand that you can create anything you want with your strong mental muscles.

Everyone has the capacity to endless development. You know that everything grows in nature, and you can grow too. There is no limit to what you can achieve. If you reach some goal a new and bigger one will instantly appear in your mind. That´s the natural growth in you too. There is no end to it, and you will never get it done. You will always be on your way to something bigger and you will always find something new to learn and improve. So never stop learning. You can build yourself to bigger and bigger success. You can be a stronger magnet all the time.

Nature knows no failure and the laws are working on everything in the same manner. To be successful, follow these laws and apply them in your life.

Now think about your goal. What you really want in life. If you move toward it, you will hit some problems and get some unexpected challenges. What happens in this moment? You will start to have some doubts and worry. And why? Because you can´t see where your good will come to you. Or how it should come to you. How you should pay your bills or something like that. Keep in mind that there are infinite resources available for you. There are infinite ways to climb your mountain. You can attract them to you, and they will help you on your way. But you have to become a magnet for them. You will not see these resources if you look too negative. In other words, there will be no magnetic force if you are polarized to the opposite of what you want.

You have the ability to focus this energy in the desired direction and align the forces, which will bring you everything you need. You can become a strong magnet for the good you desired. Nothing is impossible for nature and for you. Every mind can develop greatness. It´s only knowing how. Use your mental muscles, your talents, this knowledge, and the natural power to become a strong vibrant magnet.

All you need you possess inside of you. So learn to apply this in your everyday life. Develop greatness and you will earn richness in every part of your life. All you need is the understanding. The opposite is worry and doubt. If you see someone worry or doubt, it is because he or she does not understand these laws of being. You should understand your mental muscles and principles working in nature. Of course, never forget to apply this knowledge and practice it all the time.

## DESIRE AND EXPECT

Desire is an idea that you originate or accept from an outside source and you put it in your consciousness, and you love it. You think about it regularly and you basically fall in love with the idea. Feeding an idea means to think about it, be emotional about it, and give
energy to it. Remember that the only thing that grows is the one which is getting energy.

*"To desire is to expect. To expect is to achieve." – Dr. Raymond Holliwell*

This is when your conscious mind is in harmony with your subconscious. As a result, your body will get to a positive vibration. It means harmony and order. You are creating some strong current heading in one way, and you will be magnetized.

Anything outside of you is an effect. Everything inside is the cause. Think about the law of cause and effect. So the primary cause is always the idea held in your subconscious mind. This is dictating what kind of magnet you will become. What you will attract. This is very important so think about it.

※

Here is one example: If you see someone fishing you can observe this law in action. The fisher casts his line and waits for the fish to swallow the hook. The moment the fish bites the worm on the hook he will immediately pull the line. Well, if the fisherman does not hold the line, he will never see the fish with his eyes or eat it for dinner. Hooking the fish is the desire, but reeling it in is the expectation.

Desire is connecting to anything you want. Expectation is reeling it in. The mind is a powerful magnet, and it will attract anything which is in harmony with its ruling state.

Expectation dictates what this ruling state will be. Expectation can be a blessing or a curse. It is one of the powerful unseen forces in your life.

So do you know what regulates the state of your bank account? Do you know that other people are affected this way? If you have a business, you are attracting customers to it this way. So, what is this? You can look on two similar businesses and you will see one is full of customers and the other is empty. So where is the difference? It´s in the mind of the people working there.

We have these mental attitudes: desire and expectation which dictates the power of this force. The first part of desire must be strong and energized. We said it will connect you to what you want. If you worry or doubt, you are weakening this power. So understand you don´t have to do it. You can choose whatever you want and focus on it. You have your strong mental muscles which are helping you with it. They are giving energy and power to your desire. If there is some challenge or obstacle never give your attention to it. Do not become emotional about it. It will try to rob your energy. So be aware of it and turn back to your desire.

※

You have to be aware that you can also desire bad things. You can desire sickness. Think about the people looking regularly for something bad happening in their body. They will eventually find it. This is the law.

Your desire will connect you with the invisible part of the thing you are looking for. If you weaken or change the goal, you will miss the manifestation. If you stay constant in your desire, you will sooner or later get what you want. It will come to you. You should also understand that the thing you want already exists on some level. Yes, you can´t see it right now, but it is there. And if it is not there, you will have no desire to get it. So your desire is the proof that the thing you seek is already there for you. You only have to believe and have the faith that it will come to you. You are a creative being. You have the ability to create. This is not going to happen by accident or some random luck. It´s going to happen because you will create it. But you have to understand that and apply this knowledge.

It also doesn´t make any sense desiring something and not expecting it. Desire without expectation is only some small wishing or dreaming. It´s like hooking the fish and not reeling it in. It´s a waste of mental energy. Continuous expectation is necessary to bring your desire into life. Expectation is a drawing force of the mind which acts in the invisible realm. This is your true magnetic force! Expectation is a mental state. It dictates the vibration you are going to be in. It is creating the magnetic field. It attracts whatever corresponds with this ruling state.

Expectation creates this ruling state and governs what will be attracted into your life.

Do you realize that people mostly expect what they don´t want? Never expect something you do not desire and never desire something you do not expect. Expectation turns you into a powerful magnet. We know that a lot of people desire good things which they never expect and make no effort to grasp. They start good and get to the halfway point, but never move further.

When they finally learn to expect what they desire, then and only then can their dreams and wishes materialize.

What about people who expect what they don´t want and unfortunately this often comes true? It´s like getting a flu or cold. People usually expect to become sick once a year and they are preparing for it. They buy some medicine in advance and they have it at home. They are preparing to be sick. Really? Why are we living like that? I don´t think we want to live like that. I´m certainly not.

If you have a challenge in your life, do you expect the answer to come to you? If you are competing somewhere or you are working on some project, do you expect to win? Many desire a lot of good things but they never expect them. Learn to expect what you desire. This is the key, and this will turn you into a powerful magnet which attracts what you want.

# HOW THE ATTRACTION WORKS

There are a few steps working in attraction and we will go through them now, for your better understanding. We call the first step interest. It is like having a small filter put on our eyes and because of this filter we can only see things which are interesting to us. We can also
refer to it as our personal filter of reality. This filter enables us to see only a few things and opportunities around us.

We see in life that which interests us the most and pass blindly by other things which are of no interest to us. Let´s say you are interested in some specific thing or topic, and you suddenly see it all around you. You hear people talking about it and you find books or articles related to it. This is exactly how it works in your everyday life.

※

I remember working as a sales representative in a company producing luxury eyewear and glasses. I was learning about eyewear and what is important by choosing the right frame and shape for the customer.

I was really interested in learning it and I was looking for people wearing glasses and if they wear something suitable for them. I was also evaluating the brand and the quality of their glasses. What was the result? The first thing I saw when I met someone for the first time was what kind of glasses they wear. I was focused on it. I was interested in it. So the attraction force was showing me more people wearing glasses and a lot of different shapes and quality. I´m still doing it and I often give compliments to people with nice eyewear.

The same thing happened to me the last time I looked for my next car. I finally decided on the brand and model. Afterwards I was looking for this specific car on the market. To my realization I was suddenly seeing much more of this type of car on the streets. They were everywhere. I saw different colors, but always the same model as I was interested in. I would bet you that there were not so many of them before. This is, however, not true. I just didn´t have this filter put on before. I´m sure you have your own examples and you've already experienced something similar in your life. The big question is: What are you interested in?

This is also the place where a lot of people make their mistake. They are interested in things which are not prosperous, joyful, or healthy. They are interested in bad things happening around them and in the world. They are interested in bad news coming to them from every direction.

They are interested in daily chatter with other people complaining about their problems. They are interested in illness and economic situations around the world. Because of their interest they can't see any good around. They overlook health, prosperity, and the things they desire most. Their filter is set up and they can't see anything else. This is the reason why they fail to attract better and greater things which are all around them too. They just can't see them. They are interested in the opposite side of good. Their magnet has the wrong polarity. They want to attract good, but they are interested in bad. Think about it for a moment.

The good news is, we can change our interest. We can start to be interested in something good. You already know that you should create your new ideal mental image of what you want. It should be aligned with your purpose; with something you like to do even when you don't know how to earn money from it. Keeping your mind and focus on this new idea means that you are really interested in it. Now you have to do something about it. Without action it will be only wishing or hoping. You can see it in my examples. I was learning about eyewear and different shapes of faces and how to find the best solution for the customer. By looking for the car I was making my research according to my needs. I was doing something about it. I was interested in the car.

So, if you want to create something better in life you have to give up your old filters of the reality and build the new one. Become interested in your new idea and start to look for the good around. I also recommend giving up your old habits of being interested in those other negative interests. Believe me, you don´t have to watch TV news and complain about the current world. You can create your own. No one is to blame for a dissatisfied life, but only man himself.

You must keep up some interest and I highly recommend a positive one. You should keep your mind active looking for what you want. This will help you build the attraction. A strong magnetic power is founded upon a strong idea. This idea then directs our interest, and this flowing energy creates the attractiveness.

※

The next step in attraction is focus or attention. It means, that it is not enough only to be interested in something. You have to focus on this new idea and put it to work every day. We should give our attention to the thing we are interested in. We learned that we should use our will to do it. As we focus on our interest, we magnetize our power of attraction. We can highly increase this power having a strong interest and by our strong attention to it. It´s like increasing the electric current and the frequency of the magnetic field. This is the natural law. So use it.

Remember our thoughts stimulate interest and direct our focus. Therefore, do not think about the things you do not want. This only weakens your powers and your attraction.

The last step, and we spoke about it before, is expectation. This is like adding more intensity to the focus. This is when you believe that you will get to your desired goal. You are creating a strong belief, because you are acting on it every day and you are moving toward it. Your belief is stronger every day. It's like waiting to realize your dream in every moment. You feel it coming alive and you are excited about it.

You can't see it now, you are on your journey, but you feel it more and more. You are believing in it. If you don't believe and expect to reach your goal, your interest and focus would lack the intensity you can feel now. The moment you have a strong belief you feel a strong energy in your being.

When you believe in your dream come true, you are very interested in your work and what you are doing toward it. This interest is powered with the expectation. Through this process you will draw to you the success you are looking for. Your expectation is built on interest and attention.

If you worry, fear, or doubt that your goal will be met, you are actually diminishing your attraction power and receive less or nothing according to your beliefs. You always receive what you believe. So, the opposite side of fear and worry is understanding. You should understand that you have strong mental muscles, and you can use them to create this strong belief. Use them, employ them, and let them help you to create what you want.

Do not look on the other side and do not worry how and when. It is there. You will get it. Understand that and expect it to come in your life. Expect always the best in your life and you will have the best. This is the natural law. Nature always expects the best. Nature knows no mistake. Everything works in perfect harmony. You are part of it. Believe me and I already believe in You.

DO NOT GO BACK

Let´s say you are working toward your dreams for a couple of months, and you are moving ahead. You've also accomplished a lot of tasks and you are looking for some other and better ways to accelerate the whole process. This is normal and it should look like that. You
should feel much better and comfortable in your everyday tasks. Perhaps you meet some old friends after a while, and you would like to tell them what you are doing now. You will explain to them where you were before and how you've changed now for the better. Here is my advice. STOP! Don´t speak about it now!

You still don´t have any significant results with your new work so it could be misunderstood from your friends. They will see your challenges and feel sorry about them, but they will not understand your new direction. It means they will probably not be as excited about your new project as you are, and it could be harmful to your confidence. You can even start to doubt yourself. You have to stop it right here.

You can´t move towards what you want and speak

about the past hardships. It makes no sense, and it could put you on the wrong path. You can be proud of yourself and your new achievements and because of the response from your friends and people around you, you try to reach your goals even faster. Only to show them some quick results. Watch out. This could be a trap. You suddenly start to force some things and try to move faster investing more hours and time in your project. However, this will be exhausting, and you will be not satisfied with your progress anyway. This is exactly how we misuse our will very often.

If you are somewhere here right now, pause and slow down. There is no hurry and there is no competition. You will reach your goal, but you have to like the journey to it. Remember, that you can´t get happy results on an unhappy journey. If you feel some pressure and you are not satisfied with your progress, step back and reflect on your purpose. You are working on your idea, and you'd love this idea to come true even you don´t know how. It is not important. The important part is that you like it, and you would like to spend your time doing it and eventually get to your desired goal. It doesn't matter how long it takes to reach it. You will reach it and you know it. So stop doubting it and stop putting pressure on yourself.

Slow down and enjoy the ride again.

You don´t have to prove anything to anyone. This is your life, and you can design it according to your wants. Do not let other circumstances affect your decisions and put you under pressure. Force negates. It is better to move slowly ahead every day, rather than racing a few days and then give up. It´s like the story of the rabbit and the turtle.

※

One day a rabbit was boasting about how fast he could run. He was laughing at the turtle for being so slow. Much to the rabbit's surprise, the turtle challenged him to a race. The rabbit thought this was a good joke and accepted the challenge. As the race began, the rabbit raced way ahead of the turtle, just like everyone thought.

The rabbit got to the halfway point and could not see the turtle anywhere. He was tired and decided to stop and take a short nap. Even if the turtle passed him, he would be able to race to the finish line ahead of him. All this time the turtle kept walking step by step. He never quit no matter how tired he got. He just kept going.

However, the rabbit slept longer than he had

thought and woke up. He could not see the turtle anywhere! He went at full speed to the finish line but found the turtle there waiting for him.

This is what I recommend to you. Go ahead every day, but do not hurry. Enjoy the journey and keep in mind, you will be on your journey all the time. Be happy moving ahead and do not compare yourself to others. Also stop talking about your previous issues and problems you had. It´s not helpful and it could put you on the negative side with your thinking. Keep your magnet polarized in your desired direction. This is the key to attract what you want.

# MAGNETIC POLES

Now I´m sure you already know that our Earth also has magnetic poles and a magnetic field. We call them the north and south pole. However, they are not exactly the geographical north and south but very close to them and thus we can use them to define these positions
on earth. This is why a compass remains a good navigational tool. And again, it is also just another small and helpful magnet showing us which way to go if we look for some desired destination. It doesn´t matter where we are on the planet, a small compass can show us the way in every place. There is this magnetic field all around us. It is here for our benefit, and we should use it in our life.

    Nature knows exactly how to work in harmony with these laws and use it for her advantage. We know that some plants need more sunlight and warmth than others. If we plant those plants on the south side of a house, they will get more hours of sunlight every day. We usually build our terrace or balcony on the south side to enjoy longer hours of sunshine in our homes. Companies installing photovoltaic systems on roofs of houses choose the south side for the same reason too. This is how to work in harmony with nature. It is easy to define the south side because we know about the magnetic poles of the earth. Nature has a direction and is using this knowledge for better growth. We've also experienced those plants grow faster and stronger near strong magnetic fields. The molecules of the plant are organized in one direction, and they are growing in a more efficient way. This is what a clear direction can do for everything in our lives.

# YOU HAVE TO HAVE A DIRECTION IN YOUR LIFE

Look at your life and think about if you are working in harmony with these natural laws. What are you doing every day? Are you reacting to your environment and doing what other people told you to do? Do you know where you are heading, or do you just follow the crowd and do what others have done before? Do you know what you want in life? Is this your idea or goal or did someone else tell you that this is the right way for you? These are very important questions, so think about them for a minute.

There is no one other human being on this planet like you. You are unique and you should know it too. Your life, your goals, and desires are only yours and no other person can tell you what is the best for you. There are moments in your life when you feel it. You know what you like to do, have and be in this world. You have an idea about it, but you often push it away because you don´t know how to reach it. Here comes the biggest issue. If you don´t have this vision in your mind all the time it means you have no clear direction in your life. If you lost your compass and don´t know which way to go, you are probably going nowhere.

Following the path of others could be frustrating and you are probably exhausted every day. You are not growing.

And this is against the laws of nature. You have to grow and feel alive every day. If not, you are going in the wrong direction. In other words, your magnet is polarized to the opposite of what you want.

# TURN YOUR COMPASS AGAIN

It makes no sense to live like a puppet hanging on strings and do what others do. In fact, there are no strings at all, and nobody controls your life except you. You can do, have and be whatever you like in your life. You have the power. You are in control.

The first step to get your power back is to decide what you want and then start moving in this direction. Find out what is your true desire. Bring your vision alive and think about it every day. Desire is a strong idea about what you want in life and this idea will motivate you every day to move to it. Make a decision about what you want in life and make it huge in your current mind. It must be something which will make you smile and be passionate about it. It should be something where you have no idea how to do it. This is important. It doesn´t matter how. You only have to want it and feel enthusiastic about it. This is the first and the very important step right here and now. Make a decision about what you want and imagine it coming alive. See it with your inner eyes and employ your imagination as you learned it already. This is giving you the direction. This is turning your compass to the desired goal. This is changing your magnetic field. This is the moment when you feel good, and your magnet is polarized to what you want in life. Enjoy this moment and ask your intuition what to do now.

The second step will come to you as an idea. After you asked what to do now, look for the signs or some clues. You are not going to take a huge step right now. You are looking for some small step in the direction towards your desired goal. We should call it a baby step. And this is what you need. You don´t have to make some great jumps and hurry with your steps. You only need a small baby step every day. Something you can make in five minutes or less, but something which is bringing you closer to what you want. This is all you need. Know exactly what you want and take a tiny step toward it every day. Do not underestimate a small step. With time it will make a huge difference in your life.

From the beginning there will be no evidence of any movement towards what you want, so don´t be disappointed. It is normal and understand that it will take time till you see something new with your physical eyes. The only evidence you get from the beginning will be your feeling. This is your magnetic field gaining power right now. So, enjoy it anyway and take your baby steps further.

# GO IN ACTION EVERY DAY

Now we've arrived at one very important step on your journey to a better life. I already explained how to magnetize your mind to attract something better in your life. The natural laws are already reacting to your new magnetic power and the thing you desire is moving
toward you. This is the moment when you have to show your commitment to it.

Everything is aligned for you, but you have to do something about it to see it in your physical world. Yes, you have to make something and go in action. I´m sure you are asking yourself now, ok, so what should I do now? You are getting some ideas from your intuition or your future memory right now. The only thing required from you is to act on these ideas. Do not look for some magical new thing you come up with right from the beginning. It will be more like some very small and trivial step toward this new idea. It could start like sitting down at your computer and googling about the idea you received. Perhaps you find something interesting through your research regarding this new insight.

Remember you are looking for some interest right now. This could be the first piece of your puzzle. When you find it, you will be interested to find more about it, and you will start to look for your next piece. This is really not a big step and I´m sure you will not be exhausted afterwards. This could be the first day of your journey. The only thing you have to do now is commit to yourself that you will be looking for more pieces to it every day. I´m not suggesting putting hours on it every day. Start really small. Five minutes a day looking for some ways to move toward your idea.

You have to be patient and persistent from the beginning. Even spending five minutes a day from the start could be challenging for you. So be aware of it. It doesn´t matter how fast and how many steps you make, only commit to do them every day. That´s it! You are creating your life.

You will be moving ahead every day and you will be interested more and more in your new idea. This process will give you the power for the next challenges which are coming now to you. I´m sure you understand that to create something new and better in your life will require learning something new. It will require time. If you are learning, you will make mistakes. You will see some obstacles and your old habitual life will try to stop you every day. This also belongs to it. Be prepared for it and understand it too. If you start to put pressure on your creation or try to skip some baby steps, you will feel it right at the moment. Realize it and get back to baby steps and do it with ease. Think about the story of the rabbit and the turtle. This is the key!

How long will it take to see some results in your physical world? This is a million-dollar question. Nobody knows, but I know you will get them. I always recommend setting up a new major goal for a minimum of one year. This is your commitment right now. Work on your new idea every day for at least for a year. If you are not able to make this commitment, you are not really having a strong desire to change your life for the better. This decision must be your contract with the universe. You signed up and there is no way back to your old habitual life. If you can´t make this decision in less than thirty seconds, you are definitely not having the right goal now. It must be something you want more than anything else right now. It must be something which will create a quantum leap in your life. And, as you know, you will need a lot of energy to get there. And you can get this energy only from a big quantum leap. Remember the potential energy between your current and desired position. The bigger the distance the better and more energy available for you.

This is your action point, so do it right now!

What to do when you do not arrive at your destination in one year? First of all, evaluate if you were really honest with yourself and with your commitment to do your steps every day. Second, if you are still not there it only means that your guessing was not the best. It does not mean that you can´t reach your goal, it only means that it requires more time. This is not something bad and don´t throw your idea away because you didn´t get it on time. It only needs some time correction and better guessing. That´s all. So put a new date to it and work on it further. I´m sure you will already get some results from it and the breakthrough is only a few steps away. So, enjoy the journey further and look for your next step every day. Your desire is the proof that the thing you want is already there. Keep the energy high and your belief strong. You will get what you want.

※ We live in a world where a lot of people try to get immediate results. They want everything right now, without any waiting and without any action on their side. This is the reason why they are not moving in any direction. They try something for a week and afterwards throw it away and look for something else. They do not understand the natural laws. Everything new in this universe requires time to grow. So when people say I want it now, they are really not understanding the process.

Not knowing how long it will take to see your idea in the physical world can be really frustrating, but only when you don´t like the journey toward it. If you don´t like the steps you are taking every day, you are not moving toward your goal. Once again, there is no happy end to an unhappy journey! And if you like every step it doesn´t matter how long you are on it. You will also like the obstacles coming at you, because you know this is the sign that you are growing in the process too.

There is only one rule for you every day. Take your baby step and have fun doing it. Do not underestimate a small step in a long time period. One small step every day has the power to change your life more than a big jump all at once. Action is part of the word attraction. And constant action will increase your magnetic power too. Enjoy your ride!

# THERE IS AN ANSWER TO EVERY QUESTION

As I mentioned before, taking this new journey and walking on it will bring some new obstacles with it. There will be lessons you have to learn. So look at every obstacle and difficulty as something good. It is there to teach you something new and because of the new knowledge you will ultimately grow as a person. These are your lessons, and you will be able to find the solution. Remember you are not alone, and you can employ your mental muscles to help you on your way. Every magnet has two and opposite poles, so when you have a question, you should understand that there is also the answer to it. Without the answer there will be no question. This is a universal law. Keep this in your mind and never assume that you can´t find the answer. It is there, you only have to find it.

To reach your goal and especially the new one where you have no idea how to get there will require a new knowledge and understanding. We all learn mainly in our doing. So, taking action every day will give you a new experience and you will learn a lot in the process. There will be mistakes on your part too, so see them as an opportunity to make a correction. We can learn from these mistakes and we can avoid further mistakes in the future. So be open to making mistakes and don´t be hard on yourself for doing them.

If you have never made any mistakes, you have probably never done something new in your life. This is important to know. We are moving ahead to our destination and sometimes we are off the course. So we make some corrections, and we jump back on course. That´s all. Keep your goal in mind and check your progress every day. Are you moving toward it, or have you jumped to some other path? Try to move in one direction and avoid the distraction. The distraction can come from your old habitual thinking or from some external sources. So be prepared for it and stay focused on what you want.

## CHANGING RELATIONSHIPS

Moving to your new goal and working on it every day will start to change your awareness and your point of view. You will get more understanding every day. You will see others who are not willing to change or give up their beliefs about their everyday life.

Remember the prisoners in the dark cave. If you try to explain to them your new awareness, they will not believe you and they will not understand your new way of thinking. There will be people around you laughing about your ideas and your current work. It is quite normal, and you will understand that too. Never try to change others or argue with them. You can only understand them and their point of view, even you are not willing to agree with them. You will see that your relationship with a lot of people will start to change. Some of them will be better, because you will see them in other and better light and some of them will fade away.

There will be people who will be not in harmony with your new awareness, and you will find yourself avoiding them. In fact, if they are negative all the time, you will feel like running away every time you see them. If you have someone like that living near you, you will feel more tension in this relationship. You have to find a way to get along with them if you want or change the whole relationship. You are working on yourself, and you are improving your life. Do not let other people pull you back to the old one. The most important person in your life is you. You deserve to do, be and have everything you want. If others don´t understand that, leave them alone.

This could be very challenging and not an easy decision for you. But this could put you on the right track again and help you grow even faster. We all want to have happy relationships with others but understand it must be a giving part on both sides. To have a loving relationship with someone else you have to have this relationship with yourself in the first place. So if you love yourself, then you can love someone else too. Think about it. Reaching your desired goal will cause you to love yourself more. And doing the daily work and moving ahead will increase your self-love too.

This kind of work and stepping ahead to your goals is something that the masses don´t do at all. People are usually like sheep waiting for some direction. They are not willing to think for themselves and thus they are not moving anywhere. You will never see a lot of people going in another way than the majority. You made a decision to step on your own path and create what you want. The majority of people are not willing to make any decision, so be prepared to be alone on your journey. Build a strong relationship with your inner self and everything else will fall in place too. Don´t be sad if some people leave your life. They were there to teach you a lesson. So move ahead and learn from it. You will meet others who are more in harmony with your new way of life.

# CHANGING THE PHYSICAL

We said that your inner world will start to change. You are entertaining new ideas in your mind, and you are thinking in a new and positive way. This new way of thinking will affect not only your relationships, but you will see some changes in your physical world too. There are physical parts of you that you can´t see with your eyes or hold in your hands. They will start to change according to your thinking.

Because of the new ideas and usage of your mind you are changing your physical brain. We already know that our brain is like the switching station where the ideas connect or disconnect according to the usual pathways. We have some physical paths in our brain according to our thinking. So, if we change these old habitual thoughts we are also changing these old paths in our brain. We are actually building new connections and we are reinforcing them every day. The old paths will fade out and the new ones will be more visible all the time. Your brain will actually be changing the physical appearance. We call it neuroplasticity. You can shape your brain. This is something that scientists have already proven as a fact. So, by developing our mental muscles we are actually changing our physical brain.

I think this is really fascinating and if you understand it well, you can use it for your advantage to anything else in your life. We are talking about the physical part of you and the most obvious part of you is your body. Your thinking is also affecting your body. This is again not a new idea and yes, it is proven already. There is only one question. Do you believe in it?

Your beliefs are affecting your body.

We are approaching our body mainly from a physical level. It means when we try to change something with our body, we are looking on the physical part of it. We can make some progress doing it like that but without any change on the thinking level there will not be a permanent change. It´s like doing a diet to lose weight. We are eating less, or we exercise more. During our physical approach our body reacts but only in a small way. And usually if we stop the physical approach our body comes back to the previous state. In the case of a diet we put some weight back on.

On the other side it will not be enough to approach any change only from the thinking level.

We should combine the two. So in this case of a diet, you also have to change your thinking about yourself and your weight. You should also change the image of yourself. If you are able to see yourself healthy and with an ideal weight, your body will react better to exercise and maintain your image forever. We are more than only our physical bodies, but we are also our bodies. So, combine the two and you have your efficient action in place. We are all human beings living in the physical but also in non-physical. If you want to change something on the physical level you have to start with the non-physical part of it.

This is the key, and this is the cause of any change in your life. If you understand that, you will never have to worry or fear any more. You will know every time that it is natural, and you are growing to something better.

## YOUR PURPOSE

I´m sure you've already heard the word purpose many times in your life. And I also hear people saying, "I don´t know my purpose." Now let´s look on this word closely and understand what a clear purpose will do for you and anyone else in his or her life. We already
said before that you have to have a direction in your life. You have to have an idea of what you want and work toward it. Now, purpose means the reason why you want to achieve this goal. It also means your determination to complete what you have begun regarding this idea. And the most important part of it is your life purpose. Your reason for being and what you want to accomplish in this world.

You should know your purpose and use it in your life every day. It will help you make the right decisions and avoid the mistake of choosing a sidetrack on your journey. This is crucial for you if you want to have a happy journey to your goal. It will be a happy journey once it is in harmony with your purpose. So you have to know about it and keep it in mind. Purpose will also help you be clear and specific in forming your mental picture of what you want in life.

So much of what´s priceless about us is hidden deep inside and we rarely look there for it. Your purpose is an idea implanted in you. It´s energy, information, and power. It is in you and everything else to find it is also within you. This is something you love. Only thinking about it makes you smile, and you feel excited about it, every single time. You can imagine yourself being this person and love to spend your days working on this idea. Perhaps you spend your freetime on it.

We are all unique and all of us get some unique talents and abilities. Using these talents is very joyful for us and we like to spend a lot of time working on them. Unfortunately someone told us that we should concentrate on something else and follow some other path. They tried to convince us that our talents are not unique, and we will not be able to monetize them in our life. As sad as it sounds, we accepted their idea and left our talents there. With time we forget about them, and we think there is no way to make a living doing what we love to do. Only think about our school system. They are not rewarding someone exceptional in one field. They want us to be excellent in every field. This means we should concentrate more on the weaker parts and less on our strengths. What is the result? Mediocrity. We get only mediocre results in our lives because we are not developing our strengths.

Your purpose is your strength. You are able to spend hours doing the things you love even when you don´t get any immediate results or money from it. This is what you should do in your life. This is your gift to the world. Your duty is to develop it to the fullest and use it for your advantage.

If you already spent time working on your clear mental image or what we often call goal and you just feel frustrated, this is your answer. It is not aligned with your purpose.

*"To be successful, find out who you are, then do it on purpose." – Dolly Parton*

I hope you already know your purpose and you are working on your goal in harmony with it. If you are not sure about it, think about your activities toward your goal. Are you enjoying them? Do you have fun along the way? Is it something you like to do, or do you have to push yourself all the time? Your answers to these questions give you the clue. If you want to reach your goals and enjoy your journey it must be aligned with your purpose. If you have some issues with it, do this small exercise to find out your true purpose.

※

First of all, list ten people you admire for any reason. It could be someone living or dead.

Some people who you consider to be heroes in any way for you. They may be people you know, famous people, or someone you have never met before. Write down ten people on a piece of paper.

As a next step, write down six personal qualities or characteristics you believe that person possesses. These are the reasons he or she is loved, admired, wealthy, successful, etc. Only write down whatever comes to your mind. You don´t have to find different qualities for each of them. You probably have the same quality coming up repeatedly. It´s ok and only write them down next to the person you admire.

You now have a lot of wonderful qualities in front of you. Circle any that occur more than once on the page. If you identified them and they can occur more than twice, or many times, write them on a new sheet of paper. Now you have the most frequent qualities on your paper.

The last step is to write this sentence: This is who and

what I came here to be!

All these wonderful qualities and characteristics appeal to you because they resonate in you. You recognize them because you possess them too. You are in harmony with them. You are on the same frequency with them. This simple exercise can identify your forgotten purpose again. So use it for your benefit and understand the importance of it in achieving your desired goal.

## HOW TO BRING YOUR VISION ALIVE

We already spoke about setting your goal and choosing your ideal state. This is very important for the whole process of becoming a powerful money magnet. If you are asking how to get your vision, my answer to it is clear. You already have your vision. It´s whatever you are focusing on throughout the day. All the things you give your focus, faith, and feelings. It doesn´t matter whether it´s an image you want or not.

For many of us, that picture was not really clear till now. It was total chaos affected by outside circumstances. But now we´re aware and conscious about all of this. You already uncovered your true desire and found your purpose. Now it is time to replace the old image with your new one.

Follow these easy steps and apply them in your everyday life. First of all, form a clear and definite mental picture of what you want. You already know what you want so it´s time to be specific. Write it down and describe all the details you can see with your inner eyes. Put a date to it, when it will be accomplished. This is your part of the creative process, and it should be an exciting and joyful one. Do not think about how. It is not your job to know how. Do not think about some general ideas and concepts or things you want. Be specific and describe every detail of your idea. It´s like placing your order in a restaurant. You don´t just say, "Bring me food." You say exactly what you want and the more specific you are the more likely you get what you want. Remember that the specifics will evoke the emotion in it and your feelings will give you the power to go into action. This is the cause, and this will move the energy in the desired direction. This is energy in motion, as we call it emotion.

The next step is to think about your new idea frequently and also use your free time to do it.

You need to focus on it every day and use your will properly as you know already. You are focusing on your new idea and because of this concentration you are giving more energy to it. It

´s not about making things happen or somehow trying to force your image to come into form. It´s only about bringing more energy to thought and feeling that something can happen. We concentrate our attention and we let the energy flow. Once again, focus on what you want and not on what you don´t want! Hold to your vision and allow the creative process to happen.

This is the moment you should be calm and let your

intuition take over. You will take action on it once you know what action to take. So wait for it. Most people do just the opposite: They're out there constantly trying to make things happen the way they want them to. And you know, you can get things done that way. You can accomplish quite a lot. The problem is that if you employ this method rather than the creative one, you have to keep making things happen, keep up the pressure. That will wear you out and you will never be truly satisfied with it.

A lot of us simply lack the practice of visualizing what we desire or visualizing something really wonderful. We are all familiar with worry, which is exactly the opposite of what we want to accomplish here. I'm sure you know exactly what I mean. So rather than giving you an example you already know well, focus on positive direction. Do you remember what it feels like to fall in love? When you can't stop thinking about him or her? You have only one picture in your mind? Now, you got it. This is what I mean when I speak about falling in love with your new idea. This feeling will take you anywhere you want to go. So, focus on it!

The third step is taking mental ownership toward everything in that picture. Take possession of it in your mind. It´s already yours and have faith that it is real. Begin to act as if what you want is already a done deal. Live your new life mentally and enjoy all the things you want. See the things you want around you all the time. Some people say this idea of living as if, is only fake and not true. This is not faking at all. It´s only seeing beyond present circumstances. See it like that.

The fourth step is understanding and trusting the process. Everything has its own timetable, so let this idea grow. No one can tell you how long will it take to see your idea in your physical world. You will need faith and trust in the reality of what you cannot see yet. But it is there.

The last step is to be thankful for it all the time and expect it to take form. If you can be thankful for the things, you own only in imagination that means, you have real faith. You will create whatever you want! This part is very important, and I spent a whole chapter on gratitude in my previous book: *The Sky Is No Limit So Reach for the Stars*. You can get a FREE audiobook version of it on my website: www.petersanczel.com.

I encourage you to always be grateful and expect your vision to come alive.

CPSIA information can be obtained
at www.ICGtesting.com
Printed in the USA
LVHW080441280522
719943LV00019B/1331